A BOOK OF IRISH INSULTS

First published in 1999 by
Mercier Press
PO Box 5 5 French Church St Cork
Tel: (021) 275040; Fax: (021) 274969; e.mail: books@mercier.ie
16 Hume Street Dublin 2
Tel: (01) 661 5299; Fax: (01) 661 8583; e.mail: books@marino.ie

Trade enquiries to CMD Distribution 55A Spruce Avenue
Stillorgan Industrial Park Blackrock County Dublin
Tel: (01) 294 2556; Fax: (01) 294 2564
e.mail:cmd@columba.ie

ISBN 1 85635 254 4
10 9 8 7 6 5 4 3 2 1

Cover cartoon from *The Weekly Freeman*, London, 1924
Cover design by Penhouse Design
Printed in Ireland by ColourBooks Baldoyle Dublin 13

A BOOK OF IRISH INSULTS

SEAN McMAHON

MERCIER PRESS

CONTENTS

INTRODUCTION

The dictionary gives 'to leap upon' as the root meaning of the word inslut. The insults in this book may be taken as a collection of Irish verbal 'leps-upon', both actively (as when living up to the foreign insult that we are a belligerent race) and passively (as when these leps are made on us not only by the same insulting foreigners but also with Exocet accuracy by ourselves).

The personalities attacked or attacking are all Irish; and the places, indeed the traits, are all held within latitudes 51.5°–55.5°N and longitudes 5.5°–11°W. Some of the comments may, perhaps, not seem very insulting; in a comparable book published in England the only Irish entry is Lloyd George's description of dealing with de Valera as 'trying to pick up mercury with a fork', which many then and since have taken as an unalloyed compliment. Perhaps for the purpose of this collection of savage wit our definition of 'insult' should be meiotic: remarks and descriptions not intended as complimentary. An element of wit or justifiable rage is essential if insult is not to degenerate into mindless abuse, which is a mark not of grudging respect and worthy enmity but of hatred.

The categories are arbitrary and far from watertight, and entries within have been given in chronological order of perpetrators. Most are factual and in the public domain but some insults from fiction were too sharp to resist. As ever, the editor is limited in his choice by space, knowledge and idiosyncrasy. In this matter one can only quote a fine wielder of insult, not Irish, to the effect that anthologies (and judgements) are like Pope's watches:

> 'Tis with our judgements as our watches, none
>   Go just alike, yet each believes his own.

My thanks are due to Aongus Collins for valuable suggestions.

All versions of Irish or Latin entries are by the compiler, except when otherwise stated.

THIS LOVELY LAND

SIR ROBERT CECIL (*c.* 1563-*c.* 1612)
The land of Ire.

> Letter to the Lord Admiral, 8 October 1600

WILLIAM SHAKESPEARE (1564-1616)
'Tis like the howling of Irish wolves against the moon.

> Rosalind to Orlando in *As You Like It*: V, ii, 104-5, 1599

Of my Nation? What ish my Nation? Ish a villain, and a bastard, and a knave, and a rascal. What ish my nation? Who talks of my Nation?

> MacMorris in *Henry V*: III, ii, 110-12, 1598

JONATHAN SWIFT (1667-1745)
I reckon no man is thoroughly miserable unless he be condemn'd to live in Ireland.

> Letter to Ambrose Philips, 30 October 1709

Ireland is not Paradise.

> Letter to Alexander Pope, 30 August 1716

He gave the little wealth he had,
To build a house for fools and mad:
And showed by one satiric touch,
No nation wanted it so much.

'Verses on the Death of Dr Swift, DSPD', 1731

REV SYDNEY SMITH (1771-1845)
They do nothing in Ireland as they would elsewhere. When the Dublin mail was stopped and robbed my brother declares that a sweet female voice was heard behind the hedge, exclaiming, 'Shoot the gintlemen then, Patrick dear!'

In Lady Holland, *Memoir of Sydney Smith*, 1855

THOMAS MOORE (1779-1852)
A beautiful country, sir, to live out of!

Attrib.

THOMAS CARLYLE (1795-1881)
Ugly spectacle: sad health: sad humour: a thing unjoyful to look back upon. The whole country figures in my mind like a ragged coat; one huge beggar's gaberdine, not patched, nor patchable any longer.

Journal, 11 November 1849

THOMAS HOOD (1799-1845)
> To Scotland Ireland is akin
> In drinking like as twin to twin, –
> When others' means are all adrift,
> A liquor-shop is Pat's last shift,
> Till reckoning Erin round from store to
> > store,
> There is one whisky shop in four.

'Ode to J. S. Buckingham Esq.', 1835

BENJAMIN DISRAELI (1804-81)
[Ireland] the bane of England and the opprobrium of Europe.

Speech, 9 August 1843

WILLIAM MAKEPEACE THACKERAY (1811-63)
As there is more rain in this country than in any other, and as, therefore, naturally, the inhabitants should be inured to the weather, and made to despise an inconvenience which they cannot avoid, the travelling conveyances are arranged so that you may get as much practice in being wet as possible.

The Irish Sketch Book, 1843

JAMES ANTHONY FROUDE (1818-94)
Order is an exotic in Ireland. It has been imported from England, but it will not grow. It suits neither soil nor climate.

The Two Chiefs of Dunboyne, 1889

WILLIAM ALLINGHAM (1824-89)
History of Ireland – lawlessness and turbulency, robbery and oppression, hatred and revenge, blind selfishness everywhere – no principle, no heroism. What can be done with it?

Diary, 11 November 1866

SOMERVILLE & ROSS
[EDITH OENONE SOMERVILLE (1858-1949)
AND VIOLET MARTIN 1862-1915)]
Christopher, having cut the grocer's cake, and found it was the usual conglomerate of tallow, saw-dust, bad eggs, and gravel, devoted himself to thick bread and butter.

The Real Charlotte, 1894

W[ILLIAM] B[UTLER] YEATS (1865-1939)
    . . . my fool-driven land

> 'All Things Can Tempt Me', 1910

That is no country for old men.

> 'Sailing to Byzantium', 1927

Out of Ireland have we come,
Great hatred, little room . . .

> 'Remorse for Intemperate Speech', 1931

OLIVER ST JOHN GOGARTY (1878-1957)
Nobody can betray Ireland: it does not give him
the chance; it betrays him first.

> *As I Was Going Down Sackville Street*, 1937

MONK GIBBON (1896-1987)
    I am from Ireland,
    The sad country,
    Born, as can be proved,
    In her chief city.
    I heard much slander
    Touching her, from goose
    And hissing gander.

> 'Dispossessed Poet', 1929

LOUIS MACNEICE (1907-63)

> I come from an island, Ireland, a nation
> Built upon violence and morose vendettas.
> My diehard countrymen like drayhorses
> Drag their ruin behind them.

Eclogue from Iceland, 1936

> Why should I want to go back
> To you, Ireland, my Ireland?
> The blots on the the page are so black
> That they cannot be covered with shamrock.

Autumn Journal, XVI, 1938

EVELYN WAUGH (1903-66)

Among the countless blessings I thank God for, my failure to find a house in Ireland comes first . . . The peasants are malevolent. All their smiles are false as hell. Their priests are very suitable for them but not for foreigners. No coal at all. Awful incompetence everywhere. No native capable of doing the simplest job . . .

Letter to Nancy Mitford, 1 May 1952

PATRICK KAVANAGH (1904-67)

> Culture is always something that was,
> Something pedants can measure,
> Skull of bard, thigh of chief,
> Depth of dried-up river.
> Shall we be thus for ever?
> Shall we be thus for ever?

'Memory of Brother Michael', *A Soul for Sale*, 1947

JOHN BRODERICK (1927-89)

The city dweller who passes through a country town, and imagines it sleepy and apathetic is very far from the truth: it is as watchful as the jungle.

The Pilgrimage, 1961

THE MOST DISAGREEABLE PLACE
IN EUROPE

Anon (sixteenth century)
An Italian Frier comming of old into Ireland,
and seeing at Armach this their diet and
nakednesse of the woman . . . is said to have
cried out,

> *Civitas Armachana, Civitas vana*
> *Carnes crudae, mulieres nudae*

> [Vaine Armach City, I did thee pity,
> Thy meate rawnes, and womens nakednesse.]

In Fynes Moryson, *An Itinerary*, 1617

Anon (seventeenth century)
> Jew, Turk or atheist
> May enter here
> But not a Papist

> . . .

> Whoever wrote this wrote it well
> For the same is writ on the gates of hell.

[Notice alleged to have appeared on one of the gates of
Bandon, County Cork, and the riposte.]

OLIVER CROMWELL (1599-1658)
[Of the Burren, County Clare] There is not wood enough to hang a man, nor water enough to drown him, nor earth enough to bury him in.

Attrib. (*c.* 1649-50)

JONATHAN SWIFT (1667-1745)
No men in Dublin go to Taverns who are worth sitting with.

Letter to Charles Ford, 16 August 1725

This town [Dublin] . . . I believe is the most disagreeable place in Europe, at least to any but those who have been accustomed to it from their youth, and in such a case I suppose a jail might be tolerable.

Letter to Knightly Chetwode, 23 November 1727

Cork indeed was a place of trade, but for some years past is gone into decay, and the wretched merchants instead of being dealers, are dwindled to pedlars and cheats.

Letter to Lady Brandreth, 30 June 1732

High church, low steeple,
Dirty streets, proud people.

[About Newry, County Down, attrib.]

JOHN BOYLE
FIFTH EARL OF ORRERY AND CORK (1707-62)
The Scene of Cork is ever the same: dull,
insipid, and void of all Amusement.

Letter to Jonathan Swift, 15 March 1737

DR SAMUEL JOHNSON (1709-84)
Dublin, though a place much worse than London, is not so bad as Iceland.

Letter to Mrs Christopher Smart, 1791

Boswell: Is the Giant's causeway worth seeing?
Johnson: Worth seeing? yes; but not worth
going to see.

Boswell, *Life of Johnson*, 12 October 1779

THE CHEVALIER DE LATOCNAYE
(JOSEPH LOUIS DE BOUGRENET) (1768-?)
I arrived at Cork, the dullest and dirtiest town which can be imagined. The people met with are yawning, and one is stopped every minute by funerals, or hideous troops of beggars, or pigs which run the streets in hundreds, and yet this town is one of the richest and most commercial in Europe.

A Frenchman's Walk through Ireland 1796-1797, 1798

THOMAS MOORE (1779-1852)
[About Kerry] 'All acclivity and declivity, without the intervention of a single horizontal plane; the mountains all rocks, and the men all savages.'

Quoted in *Journal*, 6 August 1823

SIR CHARLES JAMES NAPIER (1782-1853)
[About Limerick in 1827] I remember nothing good but the pigs and gloves; and nothing pleasant but the women, who were quite delightful, and as wicked as they were pretty: or as women could wish to be.

In Sir William Napier,

Life and Opinions of General Charles James Napier, 1857

THOMAS CARLYLE (1795-1881)

Kildare, as I entered it, looked worse and worse:
one of the wretchedest wild villages I ever saw.

Reminiscences of My Journey in Ireland in 1849, 1889

ANON (EARLY-NINETEENTH CENTURY)

> I gazed on the fair one - one eye was a
>   swivel;
> Her nose it was smutty, her hands not too
>   clean;
> She told me then that she was broiling
>   a divel
> For which they are famous in Fishamble
>   Lane.

[Cork]

CHARLES LEVER (1806-72)

> Och, Dublin City, there is no doubtin'
> Bates every city upon the say;
> 'Tis there you'll see O'Connell spoutin'
> An' Lady Morgan making tay;
> For 'tis the capital of the finest nation,
> Wid charmin' pisintry on a fruitful sod,
> Fightin' like divils for conciliation,
> An' hatin' each other for the love of God.

'Dublin City' (*c.* 1826, attrib.)

ANON (NINETEENTH CENTURY)

There was an elopement down in Mullingar,
But sad to relate the pair didn't get far;
'Oh fly,' said he, 'darling, and see how it
feels.'
But the Mullingar heifer was beef to the
heels.

'The Mullingar Heifer'

DR JOHN BRENAN (*fl.* 1812-25)

A Connaught man
Gets all he can;
His impudence never has mist-all.
He'll seldom flatter
But bully and batter
And his talks of his kin and his pistol.

A Munster man
Is civil by plan;
Again and again he'll entreat you;
Though you ten times refuse
He his object pursues
Which nine out of ten times is to cheat
you.

An Ulster man
Ever means to trepan;
He watches your eye and opinion;
He'll ne'er disagree
Till his interest it be
And insolence marks his dominion.

A Leinster man
Is all cup and can;
He calls t'other provinces names.
Yet each of them see
When he starts with the three
That his distance he frequently saves.

'Provincial Characteristics', *The Milesian Magazine* 1820

FRANCIS SYLVESTER MAHONY
('FATHER PROUT') (1804-66)

Mud cabins swarm in this place so
        charming,
With sailor garments hung out to dry;
And each abode is snug and commodious
With pigs melodious in their straw-built
        sty.

'The Attractions of a Fashionable Irish Watering Place'
                [Passage West, County Cork], 1830

HENRY JAMES (1843-1916)
I was deeply moved by the tragic shabbiness of
this sinister country.

On visiting Dublin, March 1895

BERNARD SHAW (1856-1950)
. . . my sentimental regard for Ireland does not
include the capital.

Preface to *Immaturity* (1879)

. . . Dublin, that city of tedious and silly
derision . . .

Interview in the *Evening Sun,* New York, 9 December
1911

SOMERVILLE & ROSS
[EDITH OENONE SOMERVILLE (1858-1949)
AND VIOLET MARTIN (1862-1915)]
An August Sunday in the north side of Dublin.
Epitome of all that is hot, arid, and empty.

The Real Charlotte, 1894

W[ILLIAM] B[UTLER] YEATS (1865-1939)
    You gave, but will not give again
    Until enough of Paudeen's pence
    By Biddy's halfpennies have lain

To be 'some sort of evidence',
Before you'll put your guineas down,
That things it were a pride to give
Are what the blind and ignorant town
Imagines best to make it thrive.

'To a Wealthy Man who promised a Second
Subscription to the Dublin Municipal Gallery if it were
proved the People wanted Pictures' (1913)

RICHARD ADAMS (*fl.* 1880-90)
You have now been acquitted by a Limerick jury,
and you may now leave the dock without any
further stain on your character.

In Maurice Healy, *The Old Munster Circuit*, 1939

LENNOX ROBINSON (1886-1958)
Over the flat country north of Maryboro' the
watery sunshine was slanting in narrow yellow
streaks. The country there, hardly desolate
enough to be picturesque, has an air of exhaustion
about it which makes it particularly disagreeable
to me.

A Young Man from the South, 1917

George Bernard Shaw (1856-1950) by
'Ben Bay' (Benjamin T. Bailey)
(Courtesy of the National Library
of Ireland)

Brendan Behan (1923-64)
(Courtesy of G.A. Duncan)

William Butler Yeats (1865-1939) portrayed on an
Irish £20 banknote (no longer in circulation)
(Central Bank of Ireland)

Statue of
Oliver Goldsmith
(1728-74)
at Trinity College Dublin
(Photograph by
Cormac Deane)

No. 1.—This is little Chalks sent over by the London Illustrated Smudge to furnish truthful sketches of Irish character.

No. 2.—This is his model.

No. 3.—And this is the sketch he furnishes.

— **SETTING DOWN IN MALICE.**

This cartoon from the 22 January 1881 issue of *Pat*, a weekly periodical published in Dublin 1879-83, refers to the anti-Irish bias of some English cartoonists. (Courtesy of the National Library of Ireland)

Sculpture of Oscar Wilde (1854-1900) by Danny Osborne in Dublin's Merrion Square
(Photograph by Rachel Sirr)

PATRICK MACGILL (1890-1963)
God's choice about the company He keeps and
never comes near Derry.

The Rat Pit, 1915

ANON (TWENTIETH CENTURY)
    The bells of Shandon
    Sound so grand on
    The lovely waters of the Lee
    But the bells of St Nicholas
    Sound so ridiculous
    On the dirty waters
    Of Sullivan's Quay.

Rhyme chanted by visiting actors to Cork

ANON (TWENTIETH CENTURY)
The first prize was a week's holiday in Belfast;
the second was a fortnight's holiday.

Popular gibe

DONAGH MACDONAGH (1912-68)
    Bawneen and currach have no allegiance
            of mine,
    Nor the cute self-deceiving talkers of the
            South . . .

'Dublin Made Me', *The Hungry Grass*, 1947

The soft and dreary midlands with their
    tame canals
Wallow between sea and sea, remote
    from adventure,
And Northward a far and fortified
    province
Crouches under the lash of arid censure.

Ibid.

REGINALD MAUDLING (1917-79)
For God's sake bring me a large Scotch. What
a bloody awful country.

Reported comment on flight back to London, 1 July 1970

MAURICE JAMES CRAIG *(b.* 1919)
O the bricks they will bleed and the rain
    it will weep,
And the damp Lagan fog lull the city to
    sleep
It's to hell with the future and live on the
    past:
May the Lord in His mercy be kind to
    Belfast

'Ballad to a Traditional Refrain'

ROBERT HARBINSON (*b.* 1928)
Being children of a staunch Protestant quarter, to go near the Catholic idolaters was more than we dared for fear of having one of our members cut off.

No Surrender, 1960

A FAIR PEOPLE

WILLIAM SHAKESPEARE (1564-1616)
> Now for our Irish wars.
> We must supplant those rough rug-
> headed kerns
> Who live like venom where no venom else
> But only they have privilege to live.

Richard II: II, i, 155-8, 1595

ANDREW MARVELL (1621-78)
> And now the Irish are ashamed
> To see themselves in one year tamed.

'An Horatian Ode upon Cromwell's Return from
Ireland', 1650

JONATHAN SWIFT (1667-1745)

Whereas the bearer served under me the space
of one year, during which time he was an idler
and a drunkard, I then discharged him as such;
but how his having been five years at sea may
have mended his manners, I leave to the
penetration of those who may after employ him.
Deanery House, January 9th, 1739

Testimonial supplied to a servant

GEORGE FARQUHAR (1677-1707)

SUBTLEMAN: And how do you intend to live?

TEAGUE: By eating, dear joy, fen I can get it; and by sleeping when I can get none: 'tish the fashion of Ireland.

The Twin Rivals, 1702

AODH BUÍ MAC CRUITÍN (*c.* 1680-1775)

An tan téid sin le chéile i scuaine ag ól
ní féidir a n-éisteacht le fuaim a ngeoin'
tan théifid a mbéalaibh i gcuachaibh teo
béidh a ngaol le gach éinne den uaisle is mó.

[When they go out in a mob for a bevy
You're deafened with brattle like bag-
      pipers' skirls
And when they're all legless with jars hot
      and heavy
They think their relations are barons and
      earls.

'Do Chlann Tomáis' ['For Clann Thomas' (those Irish
who aped English ways)]

Dr Samuel Johnson (1709-84)

The Irish are not in a conspiracy to cheat the world by false representations of the merits of their countrymen. No sir, the Irish are a fair people; – they never speak well of one another.

Boswell, *Life of Johnson*, 18 February 1775

Richard Twiss (eighteenth century)

As to the natural history of the Irish species, they are only remarkable for the thickness of their legs, especially those of plebian females.

Tour in Ireland (1776)

Aodh Mac Gabhráin (*fl.* 1715)

A ghearráin ler chailleas mo shearc,
gabh an diabhal, is fag m'amharc;
go mba measa bhias tú bliain ó inniu,
is dar anam m'athara ní súgra.

[Useless nag, you have cost me the love
    of my life.
Go to hell, you hack without merit.
I hope you will sicken and dwindle away.
By the soul of my father I swear it!]

An bhfuil naíre ort, a ghearráin gan chéill,
a stráidh dhiabhlaí an aiméis,
m'fhágáil ar mo tharr san gcac,
is ábhar mo mhná ar m'amharc.

[You should surely, fool jade, be deeply
    ashamed,
You cretin of origin seamy!
To deliver me prone on a mountain of
    shit
In the place where my woman could see
    me.]

'Achasán an Mharcaigh' ['The Horseman's
Denunciation']

JOHANN WOLFGANG VON GOETHE
(1749-1832)
The Irish seem to me like a pack of hounds,
always dragging down some noble stag.

In Johann Peter Eckermann, *Conversations with Goethe,*
1837 [in praise of Wellington's stand against Catholic
Emancipation]

31

DUKE OF WELLINGTON (1769-1852)
The Irish militia are useless in times of war and
dangerous in times of peace.

Attrib.

SIR WALTER SCOTT (1771-1832)
Their natural disposition is turned to gaiety and
happiness: while a Scotchman is thinking about
the term-day, or if easy upon that subject, about
hell in the next world – while an Englishman
is making a little hell in the present, because his
muffin is not well roasted – Pat's mind is always
turned to fun and ridicule. They are terribly
excitable, to be sure, and will murder you on
slight suspicion, and find out next day that it
was all a mistake, and that it was not yourself
they meant to kill at all at all.

Diary, 21 November 1825

BENJAMIN DISRAELI (1804-81)
The Irish hate our free and fertile isle. They
hate our order, our civilisation, our enterprising
industry, our sustained courage, our decorous
liberty, our pure religion. This wild, reckless,
indolent, uncertain, and superstitious race, have

no sympathy with the English character. Their fair ideal of human felicity is an alternation of clannish broils and coarse idolatry. Their history describes an unbroken cycle of bigotry and blood.

Letter to *The Times*, 1836

EDWARD VAUGHAN KENEALY (1819-80)
What is an Irishman but a mere machine for converting potatoes into human nature?

Table Talk, 1875

DION [LARDNER] BOUCICAULT (1820-90)
The fire and energy that consist of dancing around the stage in an expletive manner, and indulging in ridiculous capers and extravagancies of language and gesture, form the materials of a clowning character, known as the 'stage Irishman', which it has been my vocation to, as an artist and as a dramatist, to abolish.

Letter to a newspaper in Christchurch, New Zealand, 1885

WILLIAM ALLINGHAM (1824-89)

An Antrim Presbyterian, short and spare,
Quick, busy, cool; with lancet or with pill
Acknowledged first with Aesculapian skill.
Catholicism he openly despised,
But ailing Papists cleverly advised . . .
'Ireland forsooth, a nation once again!
If Ireland was a nation, tell me when?
For since the civil modern world began
What's Irish History? Walks the child a
    man?
Or strays he still perverse and immature,
Weak, slothful, rash, irresolute, unsure;
Right bonds rejecting, hugging rusty
    chains,
Nor one clear view, nor one bold step
    attains?
What Ireland might have been, if wisely
    schooled
I know not: far too briefly Cromwell
    ruled.
We see the melting of a barbarous race
(Sad sight, I grant, sir), from their ancient
    place

But always, everywhere, it had been so
Red-indians, Bushmen, Irish, - they must
    go!'

Laurence Bloomfield in Ireland, 1864

GEORGE MOORE (1852-1933)
Democratic principles are unsuited to Ireland . . .
The Irish like priests and believe in the power of
priests to forgive them their sins and to change
God into a biscuit. They are only happy in
convents and monasteries. The only reason the
Irish would tolerate home rule would be if they
were given permission to persecute somebody,
that is the Roman Catholic idea of liberty. It
always has and always will be.

Letter to Edward Marsh, 3 August 1916

R[OBERT] M[AIRE] SMYLLIE (1894-1954)
Troglyditic myrmidons; moronic clodhoppers;
ignorant bosthoons; poor cawbogues whose only
claim to literacy was their blue pencils.

Description of the staff of the Government censorship
office during the Emergency, in Dónal Ó Drisceoil,
Censorship in Ireland during the Second World War, 1996

SEAN O'FAOLAIN (1900-91)

I have, I confess, grown a little weary of abusing our bourgeois, Little Irelanders, chauvinists, puritans, stuffed-shirts, pietists, Tartuffes, Anglophobes, Celtophiles, et *alii hujus generis*.

'Signing Off', *The Bell*, XII, i, April 1946

In Ireland a policeman's lot is a supremely happy one. God smiles, the priest beams, and the novelist groans.

'The Dilemma of Irish Letters', *The Month*, December 1949

JOHN B[RENDAN] KEANE (*b*. 1928)

    May he screech with awful thirst
    May his brains and eyeballs burst
    That melted *amadán*, that big bostoon
    May the fleas consume his bed
    And the mange eat up his head,
    The blackman from the mountain, Seánín
        Rua.

Sive: II, ii, 1959

WON'T MOTHER ENGLAND
BE SURPRISED!

THOMAS SHERIDAN (1719-88)

> Of all the husbands living an Irishman's
>   the best,
> No nation on the globe, like him can
>   stand the test,
> The English are all drones, as you may
>   plainly see,
> But we're all brisk and airy and lively as
>   a bee.

The Brave Irishman or Captain O'Blunder: Sc 7, 1743

EDMUND BURKE (1729-97)

... the age of chivalry is gone. That of the
sophisters, economists and calculators has suc-
ceeded.

Reflections on the Revolution in France, 1790

THOMAS MOORE (1779-1852)

> I have found a gift for my Erin,
> A gift that will surely content her; –
> Sweet pledge of a love so endearing!
> Five millions of bullets I've sent her.

She'd ask'd me for Freedom and Right
But ill she her wants understood;
Ball cartridges, morning and night,
Is a dose that will do her more good.

'A Pastoral Ballad, by John Bull', 1827

[written on hearing that after the defeat of Catholic
Emancipation five million rounds of bullets were sent
to the army in Ireland.]

MARY O'BRIEN (*fl.* 1783-90)

A face! for so the stories run,
Resembling much on a mid-day sun;
Broad chin, plump cheeks ascending
    rise,
Sinking the twinkling of two eyes:
Such Jacky Bull, so soft and mellow
He's a mere woolsack of a fellow.
With belly not unlike a butt,
Behold him oft in elbow strut,
Discoursing on Britannia laws,
A counsellor in freedom's cause;
As Bacchus on a barrel rides
So he on liberty bestrides,
Trotting with hobby horse's motion
To mount the cliffs of mother ocean.

Firm as a rock, a Briton born,
A foreign coast he views with scorn . . .

'The Freedom of John Bull', 1790

ANON (NINETEENTH CENTURY)

It seems that praties in their skins
Are not their only food,
And that they have a house or two
Which is not built of mud.
In fact, they're not all brutes and fools
And I suspect that when
They rule themselves they'll be as good,
Almost, as Englishmen!

'The Native Englishman (By a Converted Saxon)'

Oh, well do I remember the bleak Decem-
ber day
The landlord and the sheriff came to
drive us all away;
They set my roof on fire with their cursed
English spleen,
And that's another reason why I left old
Skibbereen.

'Old Skibbereen'

JAMES CLARENCE MANGAN (1803-49)

> I hate thee Djann Bool,
> Worse than Marid or Afrit
> Or corpse-eating Ghool;
> I hate thee like Sin,
> For thy mop-head of hair
> The snub nose and baid chin,
> And thy turkeycock air . . .

'To the Ingleezee Khafir', 1837

LADY FRANCESCA WILDE (1826-96)

> We are wretches, famished, scorned,
>   human tools to build your pride,
> But God will yet take vengeance for the
>   souls for whom Christ died.
> Now is your hour of pleasure – bask ye
>   in the world's caress;
> But our whitening bones against ye will
>   rise as witnesses,

From the cabins and the ditches in their
    charred, uncoffined masses,
For the Angel of the Trumpet will know
    them as he passes.
A ghastly spectral army, before great God
    we'll stand,
And arraign ye as our murderers, O
    spoilers of our land!

'The Famine Year', The Nation, 1845

OSCAR WILDE (1854-1900)
The English country gentleman galloping after
a fox – the unspeakable in full pursuit of the
uneatable.

A Woman of No Importance: I

BERNARD SHAW (1856-1950)
There is nothing so bad or good that you will
not find Englishmen doing it; but you will never
find an Englishman in the wrong. An Englishman does everything on principle: he fights you
on patriotic principle; he robs you on business
principles; he enslaves you on imperial principles;
he bullies you on manly principles; he supports

his king on royal principles and cuts off his king's head on republican principles.

The Man of Destiny, 1897

The British officer seldom likes Irish soldiers; but he always tries to have a certain proportion of them in his battalion, because, partly from a want of common sense which leads them to value their lives less than Englishmen do (lives are really less worth living in a poor country) and partly because even the most cowardly Irishman feels obliged to outdo an Englishman in bravery if possible, and at least to set a perilous pace for him, Irish soldiers give an impetus to these military operations which require for their spirited execution more devil-ment than prudence.

Preface, *O'Flaherty VC,* 1915

OLIVER ST JOHN GOGARTY (1878-1957)
'What shall it profit a man, if he shall gain the whole world and lose his own soul?' That must be why England gained the whole world.

Going Native, 1940

ROBERT [WILSON] LYND (1879-1949)

What I especially like about the English is that having called you a thief and a liar and patted you on the back for being so charming in spite of it, they look honestly depressed if you fail to see that they have been paying you a handsome compliment.

Irish and English, 1908

PATRICK H[ENRY] PEARSE (1879-1916)

A French writer has paid the English a well-deserved compliment. He says they have never committed a useless crime.

'The Murder Machine', 1916

PEADAR KEARNEY (1883-1942)

Oh Irishmen forget the past
And think of the day that is coming fast,
When we shall all be civilised,
Neat and clean and well-advised.
Won't Mother England be surprised!

'Whack Fol the Diddle'

ANON (TWENTIETH CENTURY)

> I went to see David, to London to David,
> I went to see David and what did he do?
> He gave me a Free State, a nice little Free
>   State,
> A Free State that's tied up with Red,
>   White and Blue.

'The Irish Free State'

BRENDAN BEHAN (1923-64)

A shrivelled-up seldom-fed bastard that had stolen money from under his dead mother's body and then put his hand on her and sworn he hadn't.

Borstal Boy, 1958

LITERARY MOVEMENTS

Sir Richard Steele (1672-1729)
We were some little time fixed in our seats, and
sat with that dislike which people not too good-
natured usually conceive of each other at first
sight.

The Spectator, no. 132, 1 August 1711

Edmund Burke (1729-97)
Because half a dozen grasshoppers under a fern
make the field ring with their important chink,
whilst thousands of great cattle, reposed beneath
the shadow of the British oak, chew the cud and
are silent, pray do not imagine that those who
make the noise are the only inhabitants of the
field – that, of course, they are many in number
– or that, after all, they are other than the little
shrivelled, meagre, hopping, though loud and
troublesome insects of the hour.

Reflections on the Revolution in France, 1790

RICHARD BRINSLEY SHERIDAN (1751-1826)
A circulating library in a town is an ever-green tree of diabolical knowledge! It blossoms through the year.

The Rivals: I, ii, 1775

JOHN O'LEARY (1830-1907)
It is one among the many misfortunes of Ireland that she has never yet produced a great poet.

Lecture in Cork, February 1886

T[HOMAS] P[OWER] O'CONNOR (1848-1929)
Our old acquaintance enables me to say that all your suggestions [for articles for *T. P.'s Weekly*] turn my stomach. They reek of Fleet Street.

Letter to Augustine Birrell (1850-1933),
Chief Secretary for Ireland (1907-16), *c.* 1902

SARAH PURSER (1848-1943)
Gentlemen kiss and never tell. Cads kiss and tell. George [Moore] doesn't kiss but he tells.

Attrib.

GEORGE [AUGUSTUS] MOORE (1852-1933)

His [Douglas Hyde's] volubility was as extreme as a peasant's come to ask for a reduction of rent. It was interrupted by Edward [Martyn] calling on him to speak in Irish, and then a torrent of dark stuff flowed from him, much like the porter which used to be brought up from Carnacun to be drunk by the peasants on Midsummer nights when a bonfire was lighted.

Hail and Farewell: Ave, 1911

BERNARD SHAW (1856-1950)

I could not write the words Mr Joyce uses: my prudish hands would refuse to form the letters.

Table Talk of GBS, 1906

JANE BARLOW (1857-1917)

That old yahoo George Moore . . . His stories impressed me as being on the whole like gruel spooned up off a dirty floor.

Letter, November 1914

AMANDA MCKITTRICK ROS (1860-1939)
His snout is long with a flattish top
Lined inside with a slimy crop;
His mouth like a slit in a moneybox
Portrays his kindred to a fox.
From his chin there drops a greasy beard,
Goatlike in hue and style I've heard;
His wrinkled neck is long and thin
To see it your sight must be in trim.

'Mickey Monkeyface McBlear'

[Mrs Ros's name for a lawyer of her acquaintance],

Ibid.

I don't believe in publishers ... I consider they're too grabby altogether. They love to keep the Sabbath and everything else they can lay their hands on.

Letters

Immoral Paris! Inside whose area are the most reprehensible dens of dignified damndom over which that immodest queen of night grins from her opalescent palace of peace, scowling over and above this abbatoir of licentiousness.

Helen Huddlestone, published 1969

W[ILLIAM] B[UTLER] YEATS (1865-1939)

He [Douglas Hyde] had much frequented the company of old countrymen, and had so acquired the Irish language, and his taste for snuff, and for moderate quantities of a detestable species of illegal whiskey distilled from a potato by certain of his neighbours.

Autobiographies, 1955

SUSAN L[ANGSTAFF] MITCHELL (1866-1926)

I've puffed the Irish language, and puffed
    the Irish soap;
I've used them – on my nephew – with
    best results, I hope.

'George Moore Crosses to Ireland',
Aids to Immortality of Certain Persons, 1908

For I took small stock in Martyn, and less
    in Douglas Hyde;
To bow to rare Æ was too much for my
    pride.
But W. B. was the boy for me – he of the
    dim, wan, clothes;
And – don't let on I said it – not above
    a bit of a pose;

And they call his writing literature as
everybody knows.

Ibid.

Æ (GEORGE RUSSELL) (1867-1935)
A literary movement: five or six people who live
in the same town and hate each other.

Attrib.

LENNOX ROBINSON (1886-1958)
It is common knowledge that the leading
newspapers employ as dramatic critics journalists
who are excellent on a racecourse or a football
field but who are hopelessly astray – or asleep
– in the stalls of the Gaiety or the Abbey.

A Young Man from the South, 1917

M[ICHAEL] J[OSEPH] MACMANUS
(1888-1951)
Said Dr Douglas Hyde
'Now woe betide!
The Gaelic League
Is full of intrigue!'

So This Is Dublin, 1927

Mr Liam O'Flaherty
Is nothing if not hearty
But his books are lacking in national
    piety
According to the Catholic Truth Society.

Ibid.

'ALGOL' (F. H. ALLEN)
(EARLY-TWENTIETH CENTURY)

They soon will come, a Celtic rout,
Athirst for blood, incensed with stout,
To throw our Foreign Culture out,
My Trinity!

. . .

Spirit of Cromwell! Rise again,
And subjugate by sword and pen
These rough, uncouth, untutored men
To Trinity!

'To Trinity' in *TCD* (1943)

MYLES NA GOPALEEN
(BRIAN O'NOLAN, FLANN O'BRIEN) (1911-66)

Is amhlaidh a bhí:

1 *doineann na dúiche ró-dhoineanta;*

2 *bréantas na dúiche ró-bhréan;*

3 *bochtanas na dúiche ró-bhocht;*

4 *gaelachas na dúiche ró-ghaelach;*

5 *seanchas na sean ró-sheanda.*

[It appeared that:

1 The tempest of the country was too
        tempestuous.

2 The putridity of the countryside was
        too putrid.

3 The poverty of the countryside was
        too poor.

4 The Gaelicism of the country was too
        Gaelic.

5 The tradition of the country was too
        traditional.]

An Béal Bocht, 1941.

Trans. as *The Poor Mouth*, 1973

BRENDAN BEHAN (1923-64) ET AL

The great voice, reminiscent of a load of gravel sliding down the side of a quarry, booms out, the starry-eyed young poets and painters surrounding him – all of them twenty or more years his junior, convinced (rightly too) that the Left Bank was never like this – fervently crossing themselves, there is a slackening, noticeable enough in the setting-up of the balls of malt. With a malevolent insult which, naturally, is well received the Master orders a fresh measure which produces a fit of coughing that all but stops even the traffic outside. His acolytes – sylph-like redheads, dewy-eyed brunettes, two hard-faced intellectual blondes, three rangy university poets and several semi-bearded painters – flap: 'Yous have no merit, no merit at all' – he insults them individually and collectively, they love it, he suddenly leaves to get lunch in the Bailey and have something to win on the second favourite. He'll be back.

'Patrick Kavanagh – A Profile', [unsigned] *The Leader*,
October, 1952

PERSONALITIES

OLIVER GOLDSMITH (1728-74)

Here lies David Garrick, describe me
    who can,
An abridgement of all that was pleasant
    in man;

. . .

On the stage he was natural, simple,
    affecting;
'Twas only that when he was off he was
    acting.

. . .

He cast off his friends, as a huntsman his
    pack,
For he knew when he pleas'd he could
    whistle them back.
Of praise a mere glutton, he swallowed
    what came,
And the puff of a dunce he mistook it for
    fame.

Ibid.

SIR BOYLE ROCHE (1743-1807)
The profligacy of the age is such that we see little children not able to walk and talk running about the street and cursing their Maker.

Attrib.

JOHN PHILPOT CURRAN (1750-1817)
Nothing but the head! [When asked by a barrister, 'Do you see anything ridiculous in this wig?']

I have never yet heard of a murderer who was not afraid of a ghost. [To a newly ennobled Irish peer of the late parliament building in College Green.]

DANIEL O'CONNELL (1775-1847)
Peel's smile was like the silver plate on a coffin.

Attrib.

GEORGE GORDON, LORD BYRON (1788–1824)
Who in soft guise, surrounded by a choir
Of virgins melting, not to Vesta's fire,
With sparkling eyes, and cheek by passion
    flush'd'

Strikes his wild lyre, whilst listening
    dames are hush'd?
'Tis Little, young Catullus of his day,
As sweet, but as immoral, in his lay.

English Bards and Scotch Reviewers, 1809

[Tom Moore wrote *The Poetical Works of the late Thomas
Little Esq.* in 1801.]

Good plays are scarce,
So Moore writes farce:
The poet's fame grows brittle –
We knew before that *Little*'s Moore,
But now 'tis *Moore* that's *little*.

'On Moore's last operatic farce or farcical opera',
14 September 1811

JOHN BANIM (1798-1844)

He said that he was not our brother –
The mongrel! he said what we knew.
No, Eire! our dear Island-mother,
He ne'er had his black blood from you!
And what though the milk of your bosom
Gave vigour and health to his veins?
He was but a foul foreign blossom,
Blown hither to poison our plains!

'He Said that He Was Not Our Brother
[induced by some utterances of the Duke of
Wellington]', 1820

R[ICHARD] R[OBERT] MADDEN (1798-1886)
'I protest as I am a gentleman . . . '

'Jintleman! Jintleman! The likes of you a
jintleman! Wisha, by gor, that bangs Banagher.
Why you potato-faced pippin-sneezer, when
did a Madagascar monkey like you pick up
enough of common Christian dacency to hide
your Kerry brogue?'

'Easy now, easy now,' said O'Connell with
imperturbable good humour. 'Don't choke yourself with fine language, you whiskey-drinking
parallelogram.'

'What was that you called me, you murderin'
villain?' roared Mrs Moriarty.

'I called you,' answered O'Connell, 'a parallelogram; and a Dublin judge and jury will say it's
no libel to call you so.'

'Oh, tare-an'-ouns! Oh, Holy Saint Bridget!
that an honest woman like me should be called

a parrybellygrum, you rascally gallows-bird; you cowardly, sneakin' plate-lickin' blaguard!'

'Oh not you, indeed! Why, I suppose you'll deny that you keep a hypotenuse in your house.'

'It's a lie for I never had such a thing . . . '

'Why, sure all your neighbours know very well that you keep not only a hypotenuse, but that you have two diameters locked up in your garret, and that you go out to walk with them every Sunday, you heartless old heptagon.'

'Oh, hear that, ye saints in glory! Oh, there's bad language from a fellow that wants to pass for a jintleman. May the divil fly away with you, you micher from Munster, and make celery-sauce of your rotten limbs, you mealy-mouthed tub of guts.'

'Ah, you can't deny the charge, you miserable sub-multiple of a duplicate ratio.'

'Go rinse your mouth in the Liffey, you nasty tickle-pincher; after all the bad words you speak, it ought to be dirtier than your face, you dirty chicken of Beelzebub.'

'Rinse your own mouth, you wicked-minded old polygon – to the deuce I pitch you, you blustering intersection of a superficies!'

'You saucy tinker's apprentice, if you don't cease your jaw, I'll . . . ' But here she paused breath, unable to hawk up your words.

'While I have a tongue, I'll abuse you, you most inimitable periphery. Look at her, boys! There she stands – a convicted perpendicular in petticoats! There's contamination in her circumference, and she trembles with guilt down to the extremities of her corollaries. Ah, you're found out, you rectilineal antecedent and equiangular old hag! 'Tis with the devil you will fly away, you porter-swiping similitude of the bisection of a vortex!'

Overwhelmed with this torrent of language, Mrs Moriarty was silenced. Catching up a saucepan, she was aiming at O'Connell's head, while he made a timely retreat.

'Biddy Moriarty *v.* The Liberator' in *Revelations of Ireland,* 1877

ANON (LATE-NINETEENTH CENTURY)

> May his toes fill with corns like a puck-
>   awn's horns
> Till he can neither wear slippers nor
>   shoes,
> With a horrid toothache may he roar like
>   a drake
> And jump like a mad kangaroo.
> May a horrid big rat make a hole in his
>   hat
> And chew all the hairs off his head,
> May the skin of a pig be made into a wig
> And stuck on him when he is dead . . .

'"Skin-the-Goat's" Curse on Carey' *c.* 1882

[James Carey was one of the 'Invincibles' who assassinated Frederick Cavendish, Lord Lieutenant of Ireland and T. H. Burke, his Under-Secretary, in the Phoenix Park on 6 May 1884. He turned Queen's evidence and implicated among others 'Skin-the-Goat' (real name James Fitzharris), the driver of the four-wheeler hired by him as an escape vehicle.]

The Times

> Scum condensed of Irish bog,
> Ruffian, coward, demagogue,
> Boundless liar, base detractor,
> Nurse of murders, treason factor.

Broadside against Daniel O'Connell

John Mitchel (1815-75)

Poor old Dan [O'Connell]! Wonderful, mighty, jovial and mean old man. With silver tongue and smile of witchery and heart of melting ruth. Lying tongue, smile of treachery, heart of unfathomable fraud! What a royal yet vulgar soul! With the keen eye and potent swoop of a generous eagle on Cairn Tual – with the base servility of a hound and the cold cruelty of a spider.

Jail Journal, 1854

John O'Leary (1830-1907)

Parnell may be the Uncrowned King of Ireland; he is not the infallible Pope of Rome.

Speech at Mullinahone, August 1885

OSCAR WILDE (1854-1900)
A man who knows the price of everything and
the value of nothing.

[a cynic] *Lady Windermere's Fan*: II

SOMERVILLE & ROSS
[EDITH OENONE SOMERVILLE (1858-1949)
AND VIOLET MARTIN 1862-1915)]
With the close of the 'seventies came the burst
into the open of the Irish parliamentary party,
in full cry. Like hounds hunting confusedly in
covert, they had, in the hands of Isaac Butt, kept
up a certain noise and excitement, keen, yet
uncertain as to what game was on foot. From
1877 it was Parnell who carried the horn, a grim
disdainful master, whose pack never dared get
closer to him than the length of his thong; but
he laid them on the line, and they ran like
wolves.

'The Martins of Ross', *Irish Yesterdays*, 1917

MICHAEL COLLINS (1890-1922)

The long 'hoor [his soubriquet for de Valera].

Passim.

Chirruping birds. This is a real nest of chirruping birds. They chirrup mightily one to the other – and there's the falseness of it, because not one trusts the other.

Letter to John O'Kane, 23 October 1921, describing some of the early moves in the Treaty negotiations.

JAMES DILLON (1902-86)

You're not a pheasant; you're nothing but a phartridge!
[Dáil response to a TD who kept mispronouncing 'peasant']

Attrib.

CONOR CRUISE O'BRIEN (*b.* 1917)

If I saw Mr Haughey buried at midnight at a cross-roads, with a stake through his heart – politically speaking – I should continue to wear a clove of garlic round my neck, just in case.

The Observer, 10 October 1982

WORSE THAN THE MEN?

AN T-ATHAIR SEATHRÚN CÉITINN
(1580-*c.* 1644)

A bhean lán de stuaim
coingibh uaim do lámh:
ní fear gníomha sinn,
cé taoi tinn dar ngrádh

Féach ar liath dem fholt,
féach mo chorp gan lúth,
féach ar traoch dem fhuil –
créad re bhfuil do thnúth.

[Jade, that's banned!
Remove that hand!
I'm just not fit
Though you're mad for it!

Look: hair's grey;
Desire won't stay;
My blood runs thin.
Yet you want to play?]

'A Bhean Lán de Stuaim' ['Woman, full of tricks']

64

ANON (SEVENTEENTH CENTURY)

Do dhúisceocadh mairbh a huaigh
leis gach fuaim dá dtig ód shróin;
a chaomhthaigh luigheas im ghar,
is doiligh dhamh bheith dod chóir.

[The dead might wake from their graves
With each honk that comes from your
        nose.
Old mate that lie by my side,
No wonder I'm feeling morose!]

'Ní Binn Do Thorann lem Thaoibh' ['The noise at my
                        side is not pleasant']

JONATHAN SWIFT (1667-1745)

'Twixt earthly females and the moon
All parallels exactly run;
If Celia should appear too soon
Alas, the nymph would be undone.

. . .

To see her from her pillow rise
All reeking in a cloudy steam,
Crack'd lips, foul teeth, and gummy eyes,
Poor Strephon, how would he blaspheme!

'The Progress of Beauty', 1719

Then, Chloe, still go on to prate
Of thirty-six and thirty-eight;
Pursue your trade of scandal-picking.
Your hints that Stella is no chicken;
Your innuendoes, when you tell us,
That Stella loves to talk with fellows;
Let me warn you to believe
A truth, for which your soul should
      grieve;
That should you live to see the day
When Stella's locks must all be gray,
When age must print a furrowed trace
On every feature of her face;
Though you, and all your senseless tribe,
Could Art, or Time, or Nature bribe,
To make you look like Beauty's Queen,
And hold for ever at fifteen;
No bloom of youth, can ever blind
The cracks and wrinkles of your mind:
And men of sense will pass your door
And crowd to Stella's at four-score.

'Stella's Birthday', 1720

MARY BARBER (1690-1757)

> Her husband has surely a terrible life;
> There's nothing I dread, like a verse-
>   writing wife:
> Defend me, ye powers, from that fatal
>   curse
> Which must heighten the plagues of *for
>   better or worse*!

'Conclusion of a Letter to the Rev Mr C-', 1734

KANE O'HARA (1714-82)

APOLLO: Pray, goody, please to moderate your
tongue;

> Why flash those sparks of fury from your
>   eyes?
> Remember, when the judgement's weak,
>   the prejudice is strong.

Midas: I, iv, 1761

Anon (nineteenth century)

For she's a big stout lump of an agricultural
      Irish girl
She neither paints nor powders and her
      figure is all her own
And she can strike that hard that you'd
      think that you'd been struck by the
      kick of a mule
It's 'the full of the house' of Irish love is
      Mary Ann Malone.

'The Agricultural Irish Girl'

So it's true that the women are worse
      than the men
For they went down to Hell and were
      threw out again!

'Killyburn Brae'

May his pig never grunt, may his cat
      never hunt,
May a ghost ever haunt him at dead of
      the night;
May his hen never lay, may his ass never
      bray,

May his goat fly away like an old paper
    kite.
That the flies and the fleas may the
    wretch ever tease,
And the piercing north wind make him
    shiver and shake,
May a lump of a stick raise bumps fats
    and thick
On the monster that murqdered Nell
    Flaherty's drake.

'Nell Flaherty's Drake'

Here lies, praise God, a woman who
Scolded and stormed her whole life
    through:
Tread gently o'er her rotting form
Or else you'll raise another storm.

In Raymond Lamont-Brown, *Grave Humour*, 1987

OSCAR WILDE (1854-1900)

The amount of women in London who flirt
with their own husbands is perfectly scandalous.
It looks so bad. It is simply washing one's clean
linen in public.

The Importance of Being Earnest: I

KATHERINE TYNAN (1861-1931)
> Margaret Grady – I fear she will burn –
> Charmed the butter off my churn.

J[OHN] M[ILLINGTON] SYNGE (1871-1909)
> Lord, confound this surly sister,
> Blight her brow with blotch and blister,
> Cramp her larynx, lungs and liver,
> In her guts a galling give her.

'The Curse', *Poems and Translations*, 1911

W[ILLIAM] F[REDERICK] MARSHALL
(1888-1959)
> . . . her face was like a gaol dure
> With the bowlts pulled out.

'Me an' Me Da', 1929

TOM [THOMAS BERNARD] MURPHY (*b.* 1935)
> . . . that hussy of a clotty of a plótha of a
> streleen of an ownshock of a lebidjeh of a girleen
> that's working above in the bank.

A Crucial Week in the Life of a Grocer's Assistant, 1969

MOTHER CHURCH

ANON (SEVENTEENTH CENTURY)

Ná thrácht ar an mhinistéir Gallda,
Ná ar a chreideamh gan bheann, gan bhrí
Mar níl mar buan-chloch dá theampuill
Ach magairle Annraoi, Rí.

[Don't speak of the alien minister,
Nor of his church without meaning or
        faith,
For the foundation stone of his temple
Is the ballocks of Henry the Eighth.]

Quoted and translated in Brendan Behan, *Borstal Boy*,
1958

JOHN WINSTANLEY (1678-1750)

Cries Celia to a reverend dean,
'What reason can be given,
Since marriage is a holy thing,
That there are none in heaven?'
'There are no women,' he replied;
She quick returns the jest;
'Women there are, but I'm afraid
They cannot find a priest.'

'On Marriage', *Poems*, 1742

71

once a year meet to show their strength and best clothes, drink muddy ale, dance with each other's mistresses, get drunk, beat each other with cudgels most unmercifully. These religious meetings are never known to pass without bloodshed and battery, and their priests often put themselves at the head of opposite parties, and gain more renown in cudgel-playing than in piety.

'A Description of the Manners and Customs of the
Native Irish', 1759

THOMAS MOORE (1797-1852)
Your priests, whate'er their gentle shamming
Have always had a taste for damning.

Intercepted Letters, or The Two-penny Post Bag, 1813

ANON (NINETEENTH CENTURY)
Scarlet Church of all uncleanness,
Sink thou to the deep abyss,
To the orgies of obsceneness,
Where the hell-bound furies hiss;
Where thy father Satan's eye
May hail thee, blood-stained Papacy.

'The Papacy' (Orange ballad)

GERALD [JEREMIAH] O'DONOVAN (1871-1942)
The Carmelites will do their best to get him. He
would be wasted on them – the boy ought to be
a scholar, not a pulpit windbag.

Father Ralph, 1913

NOËL BROWNE (*b.* 1915)
No one can seriously doubt but that the Catholic
Church has behaved to all our political parties
in an identical way as the Orange Order in its
control of the Unionist Party in the North – a
sectarian and bigoted politically conservative
pressure group.

The Irish Times, 1 May 1971

BERNADETTE DEVLIN [MCALISKEY] (*b.* 1947)
Among the best traitors Ireland has ever had,
Mother Church ranks at the very top, a massive
obstacle in the path of equality and freedom.

The Price of My Soul, 1969

PROTESTANTS WITH HORSES

Anonymous (fourteenth century)

... now many English of the said land, forsaking the English language, fashion, manner of riding, laws and customs, live and govern themselves by the manners, fashion and language of the Irish enemies.

Statutes of Kilkenny, 1366 [language modernised]

Wentworth Dillon,
Fourth Earl of Roscommon (1633-85)

The multitude is always in the wrong.

Essay on Translated Verse, 1684

Aogán Ó Rathaille (c. 1675-1729)

*Do thonnchrith m'inchinn, d'imigh mo príomh-
     dóchas,*
poll im ionathar, biora nimhe trím dhrólainn,
*ár bhfonn, ár bhfothain, ar monga 's ár
     mínchóngair*
*i ngeall le pinginn ag foirinn ó chrích
     Dhóbhair.*

[My head's all at sea, my best hope is
   gone;
My entrails are spiked; the pain turns me
   over;
Our basis, our refuge, our portion, our
   roads
Are hocked for a cent by the bagmen
   from Dover.]

   'Cabhair Ní Ghairfead' ['I'll not cry for help']

SEÁN CLÁRACH MAC DÓNAILL (1691-1754)

Brúigh, leac, a dhraid 's a dhrandal crón
A shúile, a phlait, a theanga, a tholl dubh
   mór,
gach lúith, gach alt, go prap den chamshliteoir,
mar shúil ná casfaidh tar ais ná a shamhailt
   go deo.

Cé go rabhais-se mustarach iomarcach sant-
   ach riamh,
biaidh do chiste 'ge cimire gann id dhiaidh,
do cholann ag cruimhe dá poicadh go hamp-
   lach dian
is t'anam ag fiuchadh sa gcoire gan contas
   blian.

[His sneer, yellow gums, all now turning
    to mush,

Eyes, skull and tongue, and massive black
    anus,

Every joint, every sinew, good gravestone,
    all crush

So that ne'er may be seen his duplicate
    heinous.

Though arrogant, boastful and mean all
    your days,

Your riches shall all go to skinflints of
    heirs.

Your corpse will be nibbled by worms in
    relays,

Your soul cooked in the cauldron for
    millions of years.]

'Taiscidh, a Chlocha – Ar bhás Shéamais Dawson'
[Hold Fast, Stones – on the Death of James Dawson'
    (a hated Aherlow landlord)]

ARTHUR YOUNG (1741-1820)
[Irish landlords] . . . lazy, trifling, inattentive,
negligent, slobbering, profligate.

A Tour of Ireland, 1780

BERNARD SHAW (1856-1950)

. . . the Irish squire takes the title deeds of the English settlement and rises uncovered to the strains of the English national anthem. But do not mistake this cupboard loyalty for anything deeper.

Preface to *John Bull's Other Island*, 1906

SOMERVILLE & ROSS [EDITH OENONE SOMERVILLE (1858-1949) AND VIOLET MARTIN (1862-1915)

There wasn't a day in the year you wouldn't get feeding for a hen and chickens on the floor.

'Philippa's Fox-Hunt', *Some Experiences of an Irish RM* (1899)

LOUIS MACNEICE (1907-1963)

In most cases these houses maintained no culture worth speaking of - nothing but an obsolete bravado, an insidious bonhomie and a way with horses.

The Poetry of W. B. Yeats, 1941

BRENDAN BEHAN (1923-64)
PAT: He was an Anglo-Irishman
MEG: In the blessed name of God what's that?
PAT: A Protestant with a horse.

The Hostage, Act One, 1958

The myth of the Anglo-Irish would have us believe that the most rapacious rack-renting landlord-class in Europe were really lamps of culture in a bog of darkness, doing good by stealth and shoving copies of *Horizon* under the half-doors of the peasantry after dark and making wedding presents to the cottagers of Ganymede Press reproductions of Gauguin.

Brendan Behan's Island, 1962

ACKNOWLEDGEMENTS

For permission to reprint copyright material, grateful acknowledgement is made to the following:

Tessa Sayle Agency for extracts from *The Hostage* (© Brendan Behan 1958), *Brendan Behan's Island* (© Brendan Behan 1962) and *Borstal Boy* (© Brendan Behan 1958); HarperCollins Publishers for the extract from *The Poor Mouth*, 1973, by Myles na Gopaleen); Maurice Craig for 'Ballad to a Traditional Refrain' (© Maurice Craig); Andre Deutsch Ltd. for the extract from *The Price of My Soul* © 1969 Bernadette Devlin; O'Brien Press for the extract from *As I Was Going Down Sackville Street* by Oliver St John Gogarty; Mercier Press Ltd for the extract from *The Old Munster Circuit* by Maurice Healy, 1939; Robert Harbinson for the extract from *No Surrender* (© Robert Harbinson 1960); Sinclair Howard Jones for 'Hibernia' ; the trustees of the Estate of Patrick Kavanagh, c/o Peter Fallon, Literary Agent, Loughcrew, Oldcastle, County Meath for 'Memory of Brother Michael' and extract from *A Soul for Sale*, 1947; Mercier Press Ltd for the extract from *Sive* © 1959 by John B. Keane; Colbert Kearney on behalf of the estate of Peadar Kearney for 'Whack Fol the Diddle' by Peadar Kearney; the author c/o Rogers, Coleridge & White, 20 Powis Mews, London 11 1JN for the extract from *Poor Lazarus* by Maurice Leitch; David Higham Associates for the extract from *The Poetry of W. B. Yeats*, 1941, and extracts from *Eclogue from Iceland*, 1936 and *Autumn Journal, XVI*, 1938 from the *Collected Poems of Louis MacNeice* edited by E. R. Dobbs and published by Faber & Faber; Gallery Press for the extract from *A Crucial Week in the Life of a Grocer's Assistant*, 1969, by Tom Murphy; Brandon Book Publishers Ltd. for the extract from *Father Ralph*, © 1913, by Gerald O'Donovan; The National Theatre Society Ltd. for the extract from *A Young Man from the South*, © 1917, by Lennox Robinson; The Society of Authors on behalf of the Bernard Shaw Estate for extracts from *Immaturity*, 1879, *The Man of Destiny*, 1897, *O'Flaherty VC*, 1915, *Table Talk of GBS*, *John Bull's Other Island*, 1906 by Bernard Shaw; extracts from 'The Martins of Ross', *Irish Yesterdays*, 1917, 'Philippa's Fox-Hunt', *Some Experiences of an Irish RM* (1899), *The Real Charlotte*, 1894, © Somerville and Ross, reproduced by permission of the Curtis Brown Group Ltd, London; an extract from a a letter to Nancy Mitford, 1952, by Evelyn Waugh reprinted by permission of the Peters Fraser & Dunlop Group Ltd; A. P. Watt Ltd for extracts from 'All Things Can Tempt Me' and

'Remorse for Intemperate Speech' both taken from *The Collected Poems of W. B. Yeats*.

Every attempt has been made to get in touch with copyright holders. The Publishers regret any errors or omissions in this acknowledgements notice and will be happy to rectify them in future editions.